SUPERCARS

ALFA ROMEO

Linda Hopkins

www.av2books.com

Step 1
Go to **www.av2books.com**

Step 2
Enter this unique code
SHQFTME3N

Step 3
Explore your interactive eBook!

AV2 is optimized for use on any device

Your interactive eBook comes with...

Contents
Browse a live contents page to easily navigate through resources

Audio
Listen to sections of the book read aloud

Videos
Watch informative video clips

Weblinks
Gain additional information for research

Slideshows
View images and captions

Try This!
Complete activities and hands-on experiments

Key Words
Study vocabulary, and complete a matching word activity

Quizzes
Test your knowledge

Share
Share titles within your Learning Management System (LMS) or Library Circulation System

Citation
Create bibliographical references following the Chicago Manual of Style

This title is part of our AV2 digital subscription

1-Year K–5 Subscription
ISBN 978-1-7911-3320-7

Access hundreds of AV2 titles with our digital subscription.
Sign up for a FREE trial at **www.av2books.com/trial**

SUPERCARS

ALFA ROMEO

CONTENTS

ALFA R

ROMEO

ALFA ROMEO SUPERCARS

A supercar is a **luxurious, high-performance** car. Supercars can drive faster than sports cars. Every supercar is created with extreme care.

For more than 100 years, Alfa Romeo has been carefully building beautiful cars. Not all Alfa Romeos are supercars, but each one is built with attention to detail. Alfa Romeo has won many competitions and races over the years.

It takes more than **six weeks** to build an **Alfa Romeo 4C Spider**.

In 2020, a set of **three Alfa Romeos** built in the 1950s sold for **$14.8 million**.

NICOLA ROMEO

Alfa Romeo first began in Italy in 1906. The company was then named Società Italiana Automobili Darracq. In 1910, Società Italiana Automobili Darracq was sold and renamed Anonima Lombarda Fabbrica Automobili, or ALFA for short. When **World War I** started, ALFA was going through hard times. In 1915, Nicola Romeo took over the company. Under his guidance, Alfa Romeo started to flourish.

After a period when work stopped, Alfa Romeo resumed producing cars in 1919. It was not long before Alfa Romeo began racing its cars around Europe.

Before becoming a successful car maker, Nicola Romeo owned a company that created machines for the mining industry.

MAP OF ITALY

Alfa Romeo's first factory was on the outskirts of Milan. The Alfa Romeo Museum opened near the city in 1976.

MAN-EATING SNAKE

The first ALFA logo was designed in 1910. It featured two symbols of Milan, the red cross and the snake. The word ALFA was at the top of the logo. Milan was written at the bottom. The words on the logo changed when the company name was changed to Alfa Romeo, but the symbols on the logo remained the same.

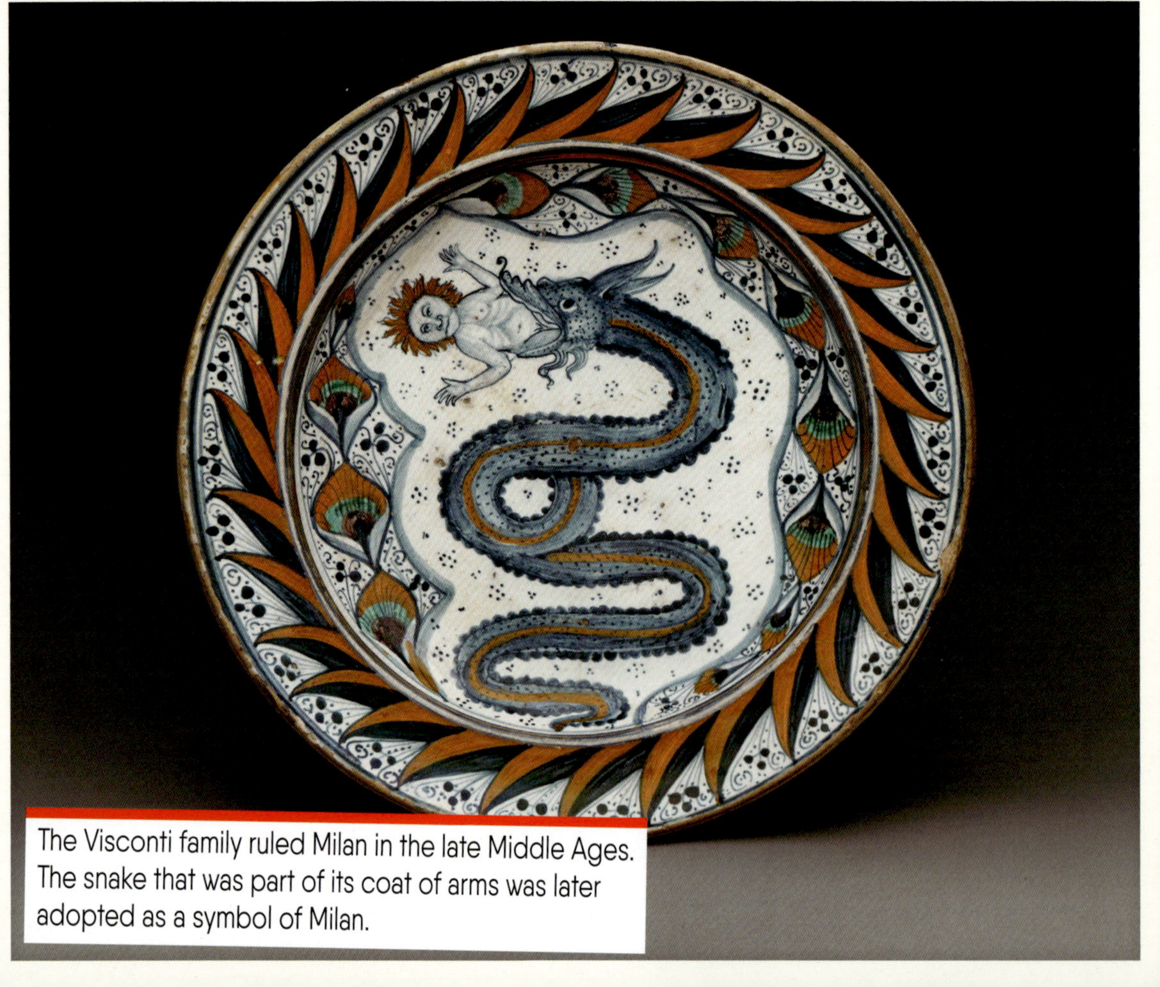

The Visconti family ruled Milan in the late Middle Ages. The snake that was part of its coat of arms was later adopted as a symbol of Milan.

ALFA ROMEO LOGO

The red cross was worn by soldiers of Milan during early wars. It is now part of the city's crest.

The snake is also known as *biscione*. It has a crown on its head and holds a man in its mouth.

The bright red and green on the gray background are used to show a bold and dashing personality.

ALFA ROMEO THROUGH HISTORY

Alfa Romeo made its name through the years as a superior race car maker. Throughout its history, Alfa Romeos continued to perform to the highest standards.

The 20-30 ES **model** is created. Used in many races, it is the first model produced under the name Alfa Romeo.

1915

1920

1923

Nicola Romeo takes over ALFA and renames the company Alfa Romeo.

Driver Ugo Sivocci adopts the *quadrifoglio*, or four-leaf clover, as his good luck symbol. In his honor, the *quadrifoglio* is added to all Alfa Romeo racing cars.

Alfa Romeo wins the first ever **Formula 1 (F1)** championship race.

FIAT, another Italian automobile company, buys Alfa Romeo.

1950

1986

2021

Alfa Romeo's racing team unveils the new C41. The car is driven by Kimi Räikkönen and Antonio Giovinazzi during the 2021 F1 racing season.

FAMOUS ALFA ROMEOS

Alfa Romeos have made appearances in many movies, including *The Talented Mr. Ripley*, *The Pink Panther*, and a number of James Bond films. An Alfa Romeo was also used in the 2019 movie *6 Underground*, starring actor Ryan Reynolds.

Former World Heavyweight Boxing Champion Muhammad Ali had an Alfa Romeo. Its number plate read "ALI BEE." This was a reference to his famous motto, "Float like a butterfly, sting like a bee."

Director Michael Bay, best known for the Transformers movie franchise, chose a green Giulia Quadrifoglio for a chase scene in the movie *6 Underground*.

Other celebrities also drive Alfa Romeos. For instance, singer Justin Timberlake drove an Alfa Romeo spider during a vacation to Italy in 2018. Alfa Romeos are also part of many collections around the world.

Muhammad Ali bought his Alfa Romeo, a 1976 Spider Veloce Series II, as a gift for his wife Veronica.

Fashion designer Ralph Lauren has a vast collection of cars. It includes a 1938 Alfa Romeo 8C 2900B Mille Miglia Spider.

One of the most expensive Alfa Romeos ever sold at auction was a 1939 8C 2900B Lungo Spider. It was sold in 2016 for $19.8 million.

AT THE RACES

From the first years of its history, Alfa Romeo has been part of the racing world. In 1933, at the **Mille Miglia**, the first nine cars to cross the finish line were Alfa Romeos. In total, Alfa Romeo has won more than 100 international races. Even when it stopped racing, Alfa Romeo continued to build race car engines for other companies.

In 2018, Alfa Romeo re-entered the F1 circuit. Today Alfa Romeo's racing team is called Alfa Romeo Racing ORLEN. It competes with the C41 model in F1 races around the world.

Legendary Italian driver Tazio Nuvolari raced with Alfa Romeo until 1937.

Before founding his racing team in 1929, Enzo Ferrari started his career as a racing driver for Alfa Romeo.

Alfa Romeo won the **first World Championship for Grand Prix vehicles** in **1925**.

Three-time F1 world champion Niki Lauda raced for Alfa Romeo in 1978 and 1979.

In 2019, Alfa Romeo test driver **Tatiana Calderón** became the **first woman** to compete in the **Formula 2 Championship**.

Finnish driver Kimi Räikkönen won an F1 title in 2007. He has been part of the Alfa Romeo Racing ORLEN team since 2019.

HOW IT'S MADE

All Alfa Romeos are built in Italy. The main assembly plant is in Cassino, in central Italy. However, some models, such as the 4C Spider, are made in a plant in Modena, Italy.

The Cassino plant has a total area of about 21 million square feet (2 million square meters). More than 4,300 people work there. The plant builds about 1,000 vehicles a day. Each car is test driven to ensure that everything runs as it should.

Nearly 1,300 robots are used in the body shop of the Cassino plant.

Over the years, the Cassino plant has produced 15 different models. More than 7 million vehicles have been made there.

It takes **47 seconds** for **18 robots** to **weld** together the **internal structure** of an Alfa Romeo.

The Cassino plant has been making cars since 1972. It was initially opened as a FIAT production line.

About **600 people** work in the plant that makes the **4C Spider** in Modena.

Cassino is considered a "green" plant. This is because it uses energy from renewable sources, and recycles or recovers all of its industrial waste.

TODAY'S LINEUP

Alfa Romeo's cars are both luxurious and fast. Some Alfa Romeos are made in limited quantities. For instance, only 500 units of the 2006 8C Competizione were ever made.

In 2020, Alfa Romeo launched a new supercar model, the Giulia GTA. This car was released to celebrate the 110th anniversary of Alfa Romeo. The new Giulia GTA was inspired by an earlier Giulia GTA, which was first released in 1965. Only 500 new Giulia GTA were put on the market.

Here are some of the Alfa Romeos on the road today.

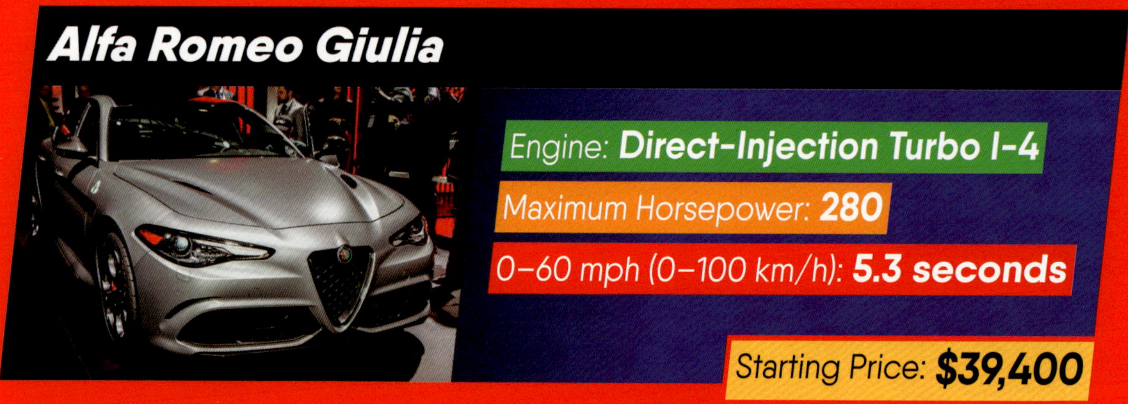

Alfa Romeo 4C Spider

Engine: **1750 Turbocharged 4 Cylinder**

Maximum Horsepower: **237**

0–60 mph (0–100 km/h): **4.1 seconds**

Starting Price: **$67,500**

Alfa Romeo Giulia Quadrifoglio

Engine: **2.9L V6 Twin Turbo PDI**

Maximum Horsepower: **505**

0–60 mph (0–100 km/h): **3.8 seconds**

Starting Price: **$75,050**

Alfa Romeo Stelvio Quadrifoglio

Engine: **2.9L V6 Twin Turbo PDI**

Maximum Horsepower: **505**

0–60 mph (0–100 km/h): **3.6 seconds**

Starting Price: **$81,640**

Alfa Romeo Giulia GTA

Engine: **2.9 V6 Bi-Turbo**

Maximum Horsepower: **540**

0–60 mph (0–100 km/h): **3.6 seconds**

Starting Price: **$171,500**

TOMORROW'S ALFA ROMEO

Alfa Romeo is looking to the future in its car designs. The company's **engineers** have created an innovative car structure that is made of a combination of extremely light materials, including **carbon fiber**. This reduces a car's weight and allows it to travel at faster speeds.

The latest Alfa Romeo **concept car** is the Tonale. This compact sport utility vehicle (SUV) is expected to launch in 2022. The Tonale is a hybrid. This means that it is powered by both a gas engine and an electric motor.

In 2020, the Tonale won the Grand Prize for the Most Beautiful Showcar at the Festival Automobile International, a motor show in Paris

The Tonale is named after a high mountain pass in Northern Italy.

All Alfa Romeos, including the Tonale, have a front grille shaped like a little shield, or *scudetto*.

The Tonale concept car was first presented at the 2019 Geneva International Motor Show, in Switzerland.

ALFA ROMEO QUIZ

1 How long does it take to build an Alfa Romeo 4C Spider?

2 How many people work in the Cassino plant?

3 In which Italian city was the first Alfa Romeo factory?

4 What does the snake in the Alfa Romeo logo have on its head?

5 Who owned an Alfa Romeo with the number plate "ALI BEE?"

6 In what year did Alfa Romeo win the first F1 championship race?

7 How many 8C Competizione units were ever made?

8 Where is the 4C Spider made?

9 What does *quadrifoglio* mean?

10 What is the name of the Alfa Romeo concept car that is expected to launch in 2022?

ANSWERS

1 More than six weeks **2** More than 4,300 **3** Milan **4** A crown **5** Muhammad Ali **6** 1950 **7** 500 **8** In a plant in Modena, Italy **9** Four-leaf clover **10** Tonale

KEY WORDS

carbon fiber: a very strong and lightweight material made out of synthetic fibers

concept car: a car built to show new technologies and designs

engineers: people trained in how to build things and use different materials

Formula 1 (F1): the highest level of single-seat car racing

high-performance: a car that is better, faster, or more efficient than most cars

luxurious: extremely comfortable, elegant, or enjoyable, especially in a way that involves great expense

Mille Miglia: a 1,000-mile-long race held in Italy between 1927 and 1957

model: a particular car design made by a company

World War I: a war that was fought mainly in Europe from 1914 to 1918

INDEX

Get the best of both worlds.

AV2 bridges the gap between print and digital.

The expandable resources toolbar enables quick access to content including **videos**, **audio**, **activities**, **weblinks**, **slideshows**, **quizzes**, and **key words**.

Animated videos make static images come alive.

Resource icons on each page help readers to further **explore key concepts**.

Published by AV2
276 5th Avenue, Suite 704 #917
New York, NY 10001
Website: www.av2books.com

Library of Congress Cataloging-in-Publication Data

Names: Hopkins, Linda, author.
Title: Alfa Romeo / Linda Hopkins.
Description: New York, NY : AV2, [2022] | Series: Supercars | Includes index. | Audience: Grades 2-3.
Identifiers: LCCN 2021022169 (print) | LCCN 2021022170 (ebook) | ISBN 9781791138752 (library binding) | ISBN 9781791138769 (paperback) | ISBN 9781791138776 (ebook other)
Subjects: LCSH: Alfa Romeo automobile--Juvenile literature. | Sports car racing--Juvenile literature.
Classification: LCC TL215.A35 H67 2022 (print) | LCC TL215.A35 (ebook) | DDC 629.222/2--dc23
LC record available at https://lccn.loc.gov/2021022169
LC ebook record available at https://lccn.loc.gov/2021022170

Printed in Guangzhou, China
1 2 3 4 5 6 7 8 9 0 25 24 23 22 21

072021
101120

Art Director: Terry Paulhus
Project Coordinator: Sara Cucini

Photo Credits
Every reasonable effort has been made to trace ownership and to obtain permission to reprint copyright material. The publisher would be pleased to have any errors or omissions brought to its attention so that they may be corrected in subsequent printings. AV2 acknowledges Getty Images, Alamy, Shutterstock, Wikimedia Commons, and Bridgeman as its primary image suppliers for this title.